Copyright © 2023 Vanessa Corpuz Francisco
All rights reserved. No part of this publication may be reproduced, distributed, or transmitted in any form or by any means, without the prior written permission of the publisher.

SCISSOR SKILLS ACTIVITY BOOK FOR KIDS AGES 3-5

THIS BOOK BELONGS TO

TIPS AND ADVICE FOR YOUR NEW SCISSOR SKILLS ACTIVITY BOOK

Each page in the workbook is printed on one side only. This deliberate choice helps prevent markers from bleeding through the paper. Additionally, it safeguards the other illustrations in the book from accidental scissor damage.

- THIS WORKBOOK IS TO BE USED WITH SAFTEY SCISSORS.

- PARENTS AND GUARDIANS ARE KINDLY REQUESTED TO ASSIST THEIR CHILD BY CUTTING OUT THE WORKSHEETS FROM THE WORKBOOK.

- AT THE BEGINNING OF THE BOOK, YOU WILL FIND PRACTICE PAGES THAT FOCUS ON LINES, CURVES, AND SHAPES.

- THE REMAINING PAGES OF THE BOOK FEATURE VARIOUS ILLUSTRATIONS FOR YOUR CHILD TO CUT OUT ALONG THE DOTTED LINES AND COLOR. THE BOOK HAS BEEN THOUGHTFULLY DESIGNED WITH CHILDREN IN MIND, ENSURING EASE OF USE. THE DOTTED LINES AROUND THE ILLUSTRATIONS ARE COMPOSED OF SIMPLE LINES AND CURVES, MAKING IT ACCESSIBLE AND MANAGEABLE FOR YOUR CHILD TO CUT THEM OUT SUCCESSFULLY.

It is crucial to provide continuous supervision to your children whenever they are using scissors. Your attentive presence ensures their safety and allows you to provide guidance and assistance as needed.

GUIDELINES FOR CHILDREN

- ASK FOR ADULT PERMISSION TO BEFORE USING SCISSORS
- SCISSORS ARE FOR CUTTING PAPER OR CARD ONLY
- HANDLE SCISSORS SAFELY: HOLD THE SCISSORS BY PLACING YOUR THUMB IN THE SMALLER HOLE AND YOUR FINGERS IN THE LARGER HOLE. KEEP YOUR FINGERS OUTSIDE THE BLADES AT ALL TIMES.
- POINT SCISSORS DOWNWARD: ALWAYS POINT THE BLADES OF THE SCISSORS DOWN TOWARDS THE SURFACE YOU ARE CUTTING, AWAY FROM YOUR BODY AND OTHERS.
- CUT AWAY FROM YOUR BODY: MAKE SURE YOUR BODY PARTS, INCLUDING FINGERS AND CLOTHES, ARE CLEAR OF THE CUTTING PATH. PAY ATTENTION TO WHERE THE BLADES ARE MOVING WHILE CUTTING.
- BE MINDFUL OF OTHERS: BE AWARE OF PEOPLE AROUND YOU WHEN USING SCISSORS TO AVOID ACCIDENTAL CONTACT OR INJURIES.
- STORE SCISSORS SAFELY: WHEN YOU FINISH USING SCISSORS, CLOSE THEM AND PUT THEM AWAY IN A DESIGNATED SAFE PLACE, OUT OF REACH OF YOUNGER CHILDREN.

Remember, practicing these guidelines promotes safe scissor usage and helps prevent accidents or injuries while enjoying scissor-related activities.

Help the bees get to the flowers by cutting along the dotted line.

Help the fish get to the coral by cutting along the dotted line.

Help the boats get to the islands by cutting along the dotted line.

Help the snails get to the vegtables by cutting along the dotted line.

Help the rabbits get to the carrots by cutting along the dotted line.

Cut me out and color me in,
I'm a circle.

Cut me out and color me in, I'm a Square.

Cut me out and color me in, I'm a triangle.

Cut me out and color me in, I'm a pentagon.

Cut me out and color me in, I'm a trapezoid.

Cut me out and color me in, I'm an arch.

Cut me out and color me in, I'm a ladybug.

Cut me out and color me in, I'm a lily pad.

Cut me out and color me in, I'm a tulip.

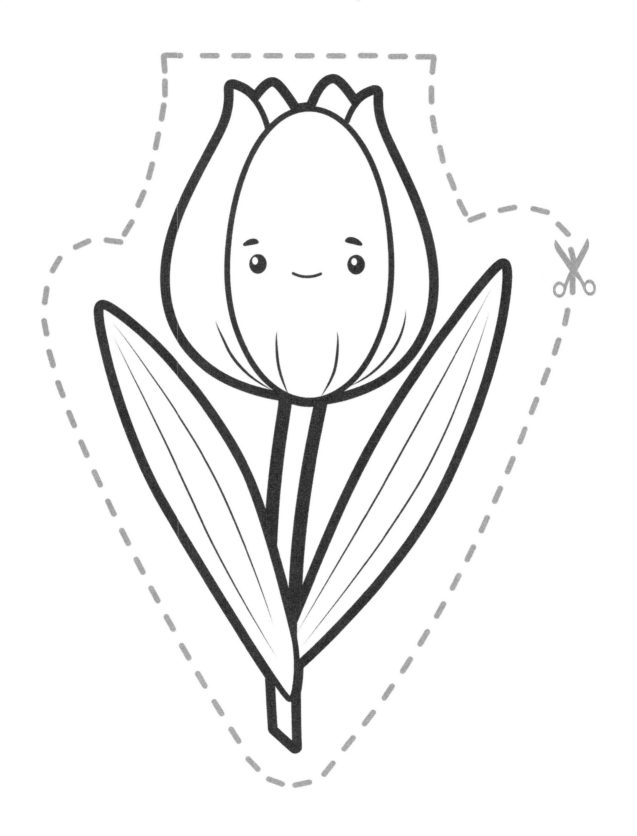

Cut me out and color me in, I'm a butterfly.

Cut me out and color me in, I'm a Rhinoceros beetle.

Cut me out and color me in,
I'm a cupcake.

Cut me out and color me in,
I'm a Clam with a peral.

Cut me out and color me in, I'm the weather.

Cut me out and color me in, I'm a pineapple.

Cut me out and color me in, I'm an apple.

Cut me out and color me in, I'm a submarine.

Cut me out and color me in, I'm a cake.

Cut me out and color me in, I'm a plane.

Cut me out and color me in, I'm a flower bulb.

Cut me out and color me in,
I'm a chick in half an egg shell.

Cut me out and color me in, I'm a dumpster lorry.

Cut me out and color me in,
I'm some cherries.

Cut me out and color me in,
I'm a mushroom.

Cut me out and color me in, I'm a ship.

Cut me out and color me in, I'm an ice cream.

Cut me out and color me in, I'm a scooter.

Cut me out and color me in,
I'm a caterpillar.

Cut me out and color me in,
I'm a cold drink.

Cut me out and color me in, I'm a car.

Cut me out and color me in, I'm a popsicle.

Cut me out and color me in,
I'm a helicopter.

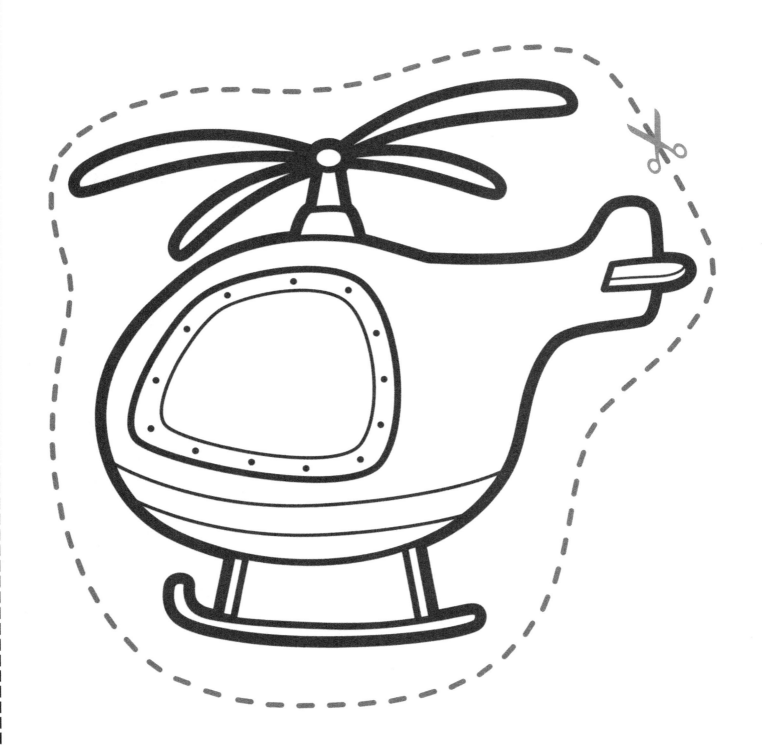

Cut me out and color me in,
I'm a broccoli.

Cut me out and color me in, I'm a boat.

Cut me out and color me in, I'm a hand.

Cut me out and color me in, I'm a tractor.

Cut me out and color me in,
I'm a hot drink.

Cut me out and color me in, I'm a bus.

Cut me out and color me in,
I'm a corn on the cob.

Cut me out and color me in, I'm a pea pod.

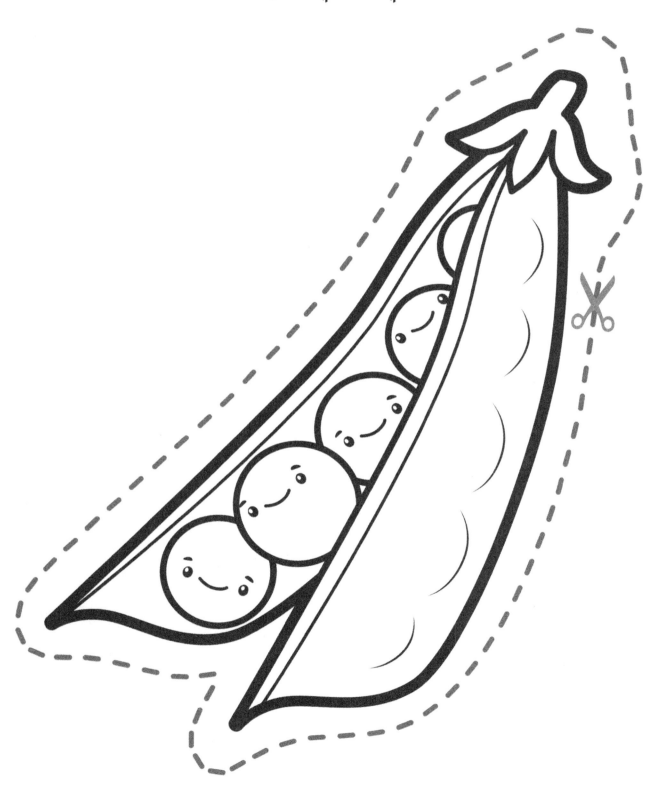

Cut me out and color me in, I'm a rocket.

Cut me out and color me in, I'm a House.

Cut me out and color me in,
I'm a Flower in a pot.

Cut me out and color me in, I'm a castle.

Thank you...

...for purchasing this coloring book.

This book has been specially made for children to help them learn how to use scissors. It includes 6 scissor skill practice sheets, 6 scissor skill practice shapes, and 38 hand-drawn illustrations to cut out.

It would mean the world to us if you could post a review. We are a small business and are always looking to improve our books, so any constructive criticism is appreciated.

Thank you again.

Vanessa Corpuz-Francisco

Printed in Great Britain
by Amazon